The Colour of Steam — Volume 8

SR BRANCH LINES

by **ROY HOBBS**

CW00328102

FRONT COVER: Former LBSCR Class E4 0-6-2T No. 32566 enters Christs Hospital station in 1955 with a Steyning line train bound for Shoreham and Brighton. This station was also the junction for the LBSCR branch to Guildford via Cranleigh, which diverged immediately behind the signalbox to head in a north-westerly direction (S. C. Townroe).

ABOVE: Former LSWR Class 02 0-4-4T No. W22 *Brading* makes a spirited exit from Shanklin station towards Apse bank with a Ventnor train in September 1964. The section of line between these points was closed completely from 18th April 1966, when Shanklin became the new southern terminus.

BACK COVER: A rare colour view in June 1957 of ex-SECR P Class 0-6-0T No. 31556 on the Kingston Wharf branch before dieselisation of this working in 1959. The line, opened in the 1870s, was worked by horses until 1938, when the P Class tanks were introduced. Up to that time the method of operation was by an inclined plane with steam winding engines from the harbour to the main line yard, where wagon turntables were installed. The system was replaced by a new spur on a 1 in 82 gradient when locomotive working commenced. Final closure came in 1968. (S. C. Townroe).

Designed by Barnabus Design & Print, Truro, Cornwall
Typeset by TypeStyle, Truro, Cornwall.
Printed by Century Litho, Penryn, Cornwall.
Bound by Booth Bookbinders, Penryn, Cornwall.

ISBN 0-906899-36-2. First Published 1989. Reprinted 1992.

Published by:
ATLANTIC TRANSPORT PUBLISHERS
TREVITHICK HOUSE · WEST END
PENRYN · CORNWALL TR10 8HE

INTRODUCTION

A wide variety of landscape and character existed on the Southern Railway system, which spanned the whole of Southern England from the hopfields and oasthouses of the Kentish Weald, through the commuter belt of rural Surrey and Sussex, via the Hampshire and Dorset heathlands to the Devon Moors and granite cottages and clay workings of Cornwall. In this publication some attempt has been made to reflect the diversity that existed and, along with old favourites, some less-featured lines have been included. No attempt has been made to distinguish between the terminal branch and secondary cross-country routes, as, in the writer's view, these both performed the similar general functions of providing a local service and acting as feeders to the main system. None of the pictures has been previously published.

The Southern Railway had continued throughout the 1930s the policy of electrification started by its predecessors, the LBSCR and LSWR; whereas they had been primarily concerned with the suburban system, their successor was intent on extending this to the main routes radiating from London. By the outbreak of the Second World War an extensive network had been developed, ranging from Hastings in the east to Portsmouth in the west. But for the war, some lines illustrated here would, no doubt, have been converted, including that from Reigate to Guildford and Reading together with the section from East Grinstead to Horsted Keynes, which now forms part of the Bluebell Railway's Northern Extension project. Both routes were shown in pre- and post-war plans published by the Southern Railway.

Fortunately, the pre-1939 developments left the web of branches virtually untouched, particularly that of the former LBSCR section, which continued to run its fleet of passenger tank engines, including the elderly 'Terriers', on rural lines within the electrified area. It may possibly have been the case that some owed their survival to company policy, as future electrification was probably viewed as the salvation for certain lines which otherwise would not have been retained — until Dr. Beeching's intervention determined their fate. One can also speculate as to how far sentiment played a part amongst railway management insofar as the retention of particularly venerable rolling stock was concerned. This is brought to mind by the relative ease with which, for example, the almost legendary 4-4-2Ts on the Lyme Regis branch were replaced in 1961 following a programme of track re-alignment. This could, perhaps have been achieved at an earlier stage, as the replacement type had been available on the Region since, at least, 1952. Further examples can be thought of, but we must be grateful for whatever circumstances allowed so many interesting machines to remain in service for so long, allowing them to be preserved for the delight of future generations. Apologies if your own favourite line has not been included, the choice having been dictated to some extent by the material available. Railway colour photography only began to gain general popularity during the late 1950s when a wider range of modestly-priced 35mm cameras began to appear on the market. However, colour film at this time was still expensive and of relatively slow speed and for this reason somewhat limited in scope. As a result, coverage of such lines as, for example, the Meon Valley and those based upon Midhurst, which disappeared in the early 1950s, has not been possible, although considerable monochrome material exists.

I would like to take this opportunity of thanking those who have loaned some really first-class transparencies for reproduction, and especially Dick Riley for his assistance and encouragement. I must also mention Sid Nash of Eastbourne who has been particularly helpful both in times past, and in connection with certain queries concerning the ex-LBSCR lines illustrated.

In a publication of this kind it is only possible to provide outline historical information or other detail, and for more in-depth coverage the reader is referred to the several excellent publications that already exist dealing with specific lines. Those from the Oakwood Press are particularly recommended in this respect.

R. Hobbs, 1989.

ABOVE: Special trains for enthusiasts were extremely popular in the late 1950s and throughout the 1960s. These often attempted to re-create typical conditions of passenger operation on lines which had been retained for freight operation following passenger service withdrawal. One such excursion over the Plymouth (Friary) to Turnchapel branch (opened 1st January 1897) took place in May 1959 and 02 Class 0-4-4T No. 30182, complete with ex-LSWR gated push-pull stock is shown at the terminus, typifying an earlier era. Turnchapel station itself was totally destroyed by fire at the beginning of the Second World War. Passenger services ceased in September 1951, with closure to freight in October 1961. (David Soggee).

GRAVESEND-ALLHALLOWS/PORT VICTORIA

OPENED:	11th September, 1882 (To Port Victoria)
	16th May 1932 (To Allhallows)
CLOSED:	4th December 1961 (Passenger)
	11th June 1951 (All: Port Victoria-Grain)

Halt to Allhallows from the former SECR Hoo Junction to Port Victoria line, had been constructed by the Southern Railway in 1932 in conjunction with a land developer, in anticipation of its growth as a significant holiday resort alongside the Thames estuary. However, this failed to reach fruition, and the caravan site together with Albany Flats and the 'British Pilot' hotel visible in this view to the rear of the station are the sole reminder of any such previous activity.

The line was doubled soon after opening to cater for the volume of traffic expected, and through coaches from London operated for a short period. During the 1950s, Summer excursions were run from the capital three times weekly, with two return workings on Sunday. (David Soggee).

BELOW: Passing under the impressive gantry at the entry to Allhallows-on-Sea station, ex-SECR H Class 0-4-4T No. 31530 departs with a Gravesend-bound train in July 1961. The spur leaving Stoke Junction

BELOW: In the bleak and isolated landscape typical of much of the Hundred of Hoo peninsula, H Class 0-4-4T No. 31266 pauses at Middle Stoke Halt with a train for Gravesend in August 1959. The push-pull set No. 481 is interesting inasmuch as it is one of those rebuilt from former SECR steam railmotor units. This halt was one of several along the line using standard reinforced concrete components, produced at the Exmouth Junction works of the Southern Railway and used throughout the system. The H Class 0-4-4Ts were prominent on passenger workings along the line through the 1950s until closure, having superseded the ex-LCDR Class R and R1 0-4-4Ts previously employed on these duties. (David Soggee).

ABOVE: Sharnal Street was one of two passing points on the line, and in April 1960, an Allhallows train comprising two push-pull units, hauled by an H Class engine, is seen crossing an oil tank train originating from the Grain refinery. The rear unit was detached here to form a short return working to Gravesend. The refinery traffic provides the main reason behind the lines continued existence, although the Allhallows spur has long since been dismantled. The section from Port Victoria, which had operated in conjunction with a paddle-ferry service around the turn of the century to Sheerness, was finally closed in 1951, and Grain became the new terminal whilst construction work was being undertaken for the new refinery in 1951. During its heyday Port Victoria experienced Royal patronage, the Royal Yacht being based there, and many of Europe's crowned heads passed through its station. (David Soggee).

PADDOCK WOOD-HAWKHURST

OPENED:	4th September, 1893
CLOSED:	12th December 1961

BELOW: The very distinctive style of Goudhurst station house is evident on 28th May 1961 as two of Maunsell's rebuilds of pre-grouping 4-4-0s of Wainwright design, Class D1 No. 31739 and Class E1 No. 31067, pass with a Ramblers' special on its way to Hawkhurst. These rebuilt engines, latterly employed on secondary main line and cross-country duties, were very popular with loco crews, being noted for their free-running characteristics. Passenger services, in the years prior to closure, were normally operated by ex-SECR H Class 0-4-4Ts coupled to two-coach push-pull sets, with goods services being in charge of the ubiquitous C Class 0-6-0s. (R. C. Riley).

RIGHT: An unidentified H Class 0-4-4T leaves Cranbrook on a dull day in April 1959 with a Hawkhurst-bound auto working. The station, which currently survives in private ownership, also played host to special trains from time to time, serving the nearby public school. These trains often used rebuilt Wainwright engines of the types depicted in the previous photograph. Hop pickers' trains were also a feature along the branch during the season, ex-SECR C Class 0-6-0s frequently being used as motive power for these workings and were amongst the last to use rakes of pre-grouping six-wheel stock, until their withdrawal in 1932, when they were replaced by the SECR 'Long Sets'. The H Class tanks were to be found on similar duties across the Eastern and Central sections of the Southern Region in their final years. Fortunately, one-time branch engine No. 31263 survived to be preserved on the Bluebell Railway, where it can now be seen in the full glory of its SECR colour scheme. (David Soggee).

LEFT: The tail lamp is in the process of being repositioned at the opposite end of the train (Set 732, made up of former SECR short wheelbase stock) following its arrival at the Hawkhurst terminus in August 1959. Unseen H Class No. 31512 is the motive power. Hawkhurst station, in common with others on the branch, was notorious for being some considerable distance from the community it was built to serve, and in this particular instance a journey of some two miles was involved, being mainly uphill to the town centre! Such factors, no doubt, helped contribute to its early demise, along with so many other branch lines during the Beeching period. (David Soggee).

REDHILL-GUILDFORD

OPENED:	15th October, 1849

BELOW: Whilst the signalman secures the crossing gates protecting the secondary road from Betchworth via Pebble Hill towards Sutton, former SR Maunsell N Class 2-6-0 No. 31852, against the background of the North Downs ridge, leaves Betchworth station with the 4.04 pm from Redhill-Reading in May 1963. These engines were the mainstay of both passenger and freight traffic for many years during the 1950s and 1960s, the former especially following the withdrawal of the mainly ex-SECR pre-grouping classes of 4-4-0s which had operated previously, and the transfer of the standard Class 4MT 2-6-0s which succeeded them for a short period. The goods yard was still in use for coal traffic at this time, whilst the siding on the left, though then disused, served The Betchworth Greystone Lime Co., which owned several unique industrial locomotives on two gauges, most of which are now preserved. Former SECR D Class 4-4-0 No. 737, similarly now preserved, was typical of the 4-4-0s which previously worked over the line and was in fact, one of those so employed during BR days. It is probably not generally known that the line was used for film purposes in the mid-1940s, when an up running loop line at the now long-defunct Buckland Sidings featured in the opening scenes of the film 'Frieda', depicting the escape of refugees from occupied Poland. For this purpose a suitably disguised WD 2-8-0 was employed.

ABOVE: Approaching Betchworth in May 1963 with a mixed rake of Maunsell-designed (narrow Restriction 'I') Hastings line stock is U Class 2-6-0 No. 31618 with a train in the Redhill direction. Engines of this type worked alongside the smaller-wheeled N Class on these services. The U Class with larger 6ft 0in diameter driving wheels, totalled fifty engines, and originated with the rebuilding of the Maunsell-designed K Class River 2-6-4Ts following the Sevenoaks accident in 1927, though 30, including No. 31618, were built from new. The original intention had been to build further River tanks, and the engine was to have been named *River Hamble* under this programme. Restored to earlier SR condition, albeit with Standard chimney and altered front-end arrangements, it is now preserved on the Bluebell Railway. During the Summer period until 1962, the line was used extensively by holiday trains from the Midlands to South Coast resorts, these being invariably hauled to Redhill by ex-GWR '43xx' Class 2-6-0s or, latterly, '78xx' Manor Class 4-6-0s.

BELOW: Shalford is the location of this October 1964 picture, which shows Standard Class 4MT 2-6-4T No. 80145 leaving the station with a Reading train consisting of former Hastings line narrow-width stock, towards the close of steam operation on the line. This came to an end on 2nd January 1965, when hybrid 3-car DMUs were brought in as replacement. These were formed from the combination of two Hastings narrow vehicles comprising driving and trailer coaches, plus an additional driving trailer from redundant electric stock. Due to the combination of one standard and two narrow-width vehicles, these units were christened 'Tadpoles' by the operating staff! Note the banner repeater signal, presumably installed as a result of sighting difficulties, immediately before the road bridge and visible above the third carriage.

ABOVE: Standard Class 4MT 2-6-0 No. 76031 approaches Shalford in October 1964 with a train for Redhill, shortly after crossing the River Wey by the distinctive girder bridge seen in the middle distance, having left the main Waterloo-Portsmouth route at Shalford Junction, just out of sight to the right of this bridge. The clump of trees immediately behind the train marks the start of earthworks of an uncompleted spur, intended to connect the Redhill and Portsmouth lines. Work was started around 1858 with the intention of persuading either the LSWR or SER to take an interest in the Portsmouth Direct line, which had been constructed as a speculative venture by the railway entrepreneur Thomas Brassey. The LSWR finally decided that line purchase would

be to their advantage in the face of the possible SER threat. The earthworks much overgrown, are still visible from the line.
No. 76031 which, unusually, appears to be carrying the headcode for Reading to Margate via Redhill, was until 1962 an Eastern Region engine based at March (Code 31B), and used on M&GNJR services. For this reason a tablet-catcher was required, and the recess in the cab side sheets shows where such equipment had been previously mounted. History was being repeated as, for a time in the late 1950s, a batch of these engines, (Nos. 76053-76062), had been allocated to Redhill shed from new, and regularly worked the route.

OXTED-ASHURST JUNCTION

OPENED:	1st October, 1888

BELOW: This line, which diverged from that from South Croydon to Crowhurst at Hurst Green Junction below Oxted, formed a shorter route to Tunbridge Wells than that via East Grinstead, and local services from Oxted were latterly provided by push-pull auto trains. Through services from London to Brighton via Eridge also used the route, and recent closures have resulted in it being combined with the remaining portion of the Eridge-Lewes line, becoming a section of the Uckfield branch. In the snowy landscape which characterised the Winter of 1963, H Class 0-4-4T No. 31005 leaves Edenbridge Town during February with an Oxted-Tunbridge Wells West motor train. During the autumn of 1959 these services were bedevilled with motive power problems, with the result that from time to time one could find variously C Class 0-6-0s or 4-4-0s of Classes D1 or L employed on the two-coach motor sets!

LEFT: Ashurst station with a former LSWR Class M7 No. 30055 approaching on an Oxted-bound train with Maunsell push-pull set 604 in May 1963. Note the open palisaded signal frame, of which an example also existed at one time at Sheffield Park, now headquarters of the Bluebell Railway. Dieselisation of these services, along with other Oxted line workings, was completed during the Autumn of 1963. (David Soggee).

RIGHT: Another view of Ashurst station, this time in September 1962, showing the delightful Sussex Wealden countryside through which the line passed. Set 604 is again featured, now with an unidentified H Class tank leaving on a Tunbridge Wells West train. A box van of LSWR origin is visible in the down siding. During the early 1960s, one business train from London, the 4.48 pm from Victoria, was worked to this point and divided, a locomotive being provided to take the rear portion to Tunbridge Wells West, whilst the 4-coach forward section carried on to Brighton. Various types of engine were used, but the main train was usually hauled by a Maunsell Class U1 2-6-0 or latterly a Standard Class 4MT 2-6-4T, the Tunbridge Wells section being taken forward by various six-coupled locomotives including on occasions by a Q Class 0-6-0.

THREE BRIDGES-EAST GRINSTEAD

OPENED:	9th July 1855
CLOSED:	2nd November 1967 (Passenger)

BELOW: Former LSWR Class M7 0-4-4T No. 30133 bustles along near Worth, close to the famous Worth Abbey with a Three Bridges to East Grinstead working in March 1963. The coaching stock comprises one of the push-pull sets converted from Maunsell vehicles, which superseded various units of pre-grouping origin, these all being finally withdrawn in around 1962. The M7s were not universally popular with their crews (due particularly to difficulties in oiling-round their inside motion), compared with the ex-SECR H Class 0-4-4Ts also employed. At this point the engine has just commenced the climb to Compasses Crossing near Rowfant Station. Diesel traction was introduced in June 1963 when 3-car DMUs from the Oxted Lines scheme replaced the majority of steam services.

ABOVE: Rowfant, one of two intermediate stations on the branch, showing H Class No. 31530 with an East Grinstead train on 21st February 1960. To judge by its appearance, the engine is in ex-works condition as the various markings for the connections allowing auto-train operation are still clearly shown on the front buffer beam. Sidings existed here to serve a government-controlled fuel depot, which resulted in the infrequent operation of block tanker trains. At East Grinstead the High Level station was situated on a bridge crossing the Low Level platforms. When the High Level was closed following withdrawal of services, one platform was retained to allow Low Level platform interchange, this resulting in its description as 'the Southerns most expensive footbridge'! (David Soggee).

EAST GRINSTEAD-LEWES (CULVER JUNCTION)

OPENED:	1st August 1882
CLOSED:	17th March 1958 (see text)

BELOW: Former LBSCR Class C2X 0-6-0 No. 32442 is shown at East Grinstead (L.L.) having detached from a freight working originating at Norwood Junction. What is most probably a train for Three Bridges can be seen occupying the High Level platform, referred to earlier, immediately behind the engine. A freight spur to the High Level yard existed several feet to the right of the siding shown in the foreground. This view was taken just before the final closure in March 1958. The Bluebell Railway is at the time of writing, in the process of re-establishing the line through from Horsted Keynes, and will be using the Low Level yard site, just out of view to the right, for its new terminus. The original station has now been demolished and replaced by a basic permanent structure of 'box-cabin' design. (R. C. Riley).

BOTTOM: Now world-famous as the HQ of the Bluebell Railway, Sheffield Park is shown here on 30th April 1955 (just before first closure), with No. 42081, one of several LMS-designed 2-6-4Ts built at Brighton, on a Lewes train comprising one of the former SECR 'Birdcage Triple' sets, once common on lines in south-east England. Initial closure took effect on 29th May 1955, but was subsequently found to be illegal, contravening the terms of the original Parliamentary Act. Limited services were therefore restored from August 1956 until March 1958 when final closure took place. The intervening service provided by BR was an extremely reluctant one, those stations not shown in the Act (ie Kingscote and Barcombe) not being reopened; whilst one engine and coach formed the basis of the four services legally required each way. A variety of locomotives were provided during this time, but ex-LBSCR E4 Class 0-6-2Ts and C2X Class 0-6-0s would appear to have predominated. (R. C. Riley).

CHRISTS HOSPITAL (Itchingfield Junction)-SHOREHAM

OPENED:	16th September 1861
CLOSED:	7th March 1966 (Passengers)
	1st May 1980 (Freight: Beeding Cement Works-Shoreham)

BELOW: During the final weeks of freight working along the whole length of the line between Christs Hospital and Shoreham via Steyning, SR Q Class 0-6-0 No. 30547 engages in shunting at Southwater in May 1962. The local brickworks siding can be seen in the middle distance diverging from the yard loop. Passenger services in the years up to closure were provided by Ivatt Class 2MT 2-6-2Ts of LMS design, where previous to their introduction, ex-LBSCR 0-6-2Ts of Class E4 had dealt with the majority of workings (see cover). For a few Sundays in April 1964, the line had been the return route for 'The Regency Belle', a privately-sponsored Pullman excursion, run from Victoria to Brighton on Saturday evenings for theatregoers and night-club patrons at this south coast resort. Engineering works on the main line required the use of this unusual route for the return working to London in the early hours of Sunday morning, and Bulleid Light Pacifics were the regular power on the few occasions this train ran.

CHRISTS HOSPITAL-GUILDFORD (Peasmarsh Junction)

OPENED:	2nd October 1865
CLOSED:	14th June 1965

BELOW: Ivatt Class 2MT 2-6-2T No. 41294 departs Slinfold in June 1965 with a train for Guildford via Cranleigh. The signal arm on the LBSCR-pattern wooden post has been replaced with one of standard SR upper quadrant design. In earlier years, Brighton 0-4-4Ts of Class D3 were often employed along the line. Following the withdrawal of the class in the early 1950s, locomotives of Classes M7 and H, in conjunction with two-coach push-pull units, took over the running until they were replaced by the LMS-designed 2-6-2Ts on Bulleid three-coach sets. Class D3 No. 32390, which survived the remainder of its sisters by three years, undertook a final sentimental working on the branch in September 1955, being despatched to Ashford for scrapping some four days later.

LEFT: Rudgwick station in June 1965 with No. 41294 shown departing on a Horsham train. Until closure of the yard, considerable coal traffic was handled here. The branch was popular with ramblers and special trains were periodically run for them in post-war years. Continuing a pre-war tradition, through excursions from Reading to Brighton operated regularly in the 1950s and early 1960s, these necessitating an engine change and reversal at Horsham, due to the direction of running. For a short period following the opening in 1865, a spur just over half-mile in length, had been constructed at the Stammerham Junction, later Christs Hospital, end to enable direct access to the Shoreham line, but this was closed in 1867 due to lack of use. The earthworks of this line were still visible as late as the 1950s.

RIGHT: The most well-known station along the line was Baynards, which, built specifically to serve the large estate of Baynards Park adjacent to the line, was otherwise fairly isolated. One of the staff gained a considerable reputation for his dahlia growing capabilities and the whole station area was a sight to behold at the height of the season. It was also notable for having alongside, an extremely small public house, possibly a converted cottage, called 'The Thurlow Arms', whose sign can just be seen in the right of this view, which was in the charge of two retired ladies. Not surprisingly they very quickly ran out of refreshments when this last special train stopped for photographic purposes, on a warm 13th June 1965!

Motive power was provided by two Bulleid 0-6-0s of Class Q1, Nos. 33006 and 33027. This class had been built during the Second World War, when limitations on the use of materials resulted in their rather unusual and modernistic appearance. They were very efficient machines, however, and lasted until the very end of Southern Region steam in 1967, on both freight and occasional passenger duties. This station achieved a measure of fame in 1957 when it was the location for the first TV production of 'The Railway Children'. Deposits of Fullers Earth were also quarried locally, and provided much of the freight traffic.

HAVANT-HAYLING ISLAND

OPENED:	17th July 1867
CLOSED:	4th November 1963

BELOW: With a well-filled train of holidaymakers in August 1963, ex-LBSCR Stroudley 'Terrier' AIX Class 0-6-0T No. 32670 climbs away from Havant, at the start of its journey to Hayling Island. The branch was the last outpost of passenger train operation for these engines, which had been designed in the 1870s for use on the LBSCR Company's London suburban routes. Many of them were approaching a century of service at the time of withdrawal. This was subsequently achieved by several under private ownership, the majority of those remaining at withdrawal having been purchased by the preservation movement.

ABOVE: Again in August 1963, No. 32670 approaches Langstone Halt across Langstone road crossing, whilst the crossing keeper prepares for the rapid release of the gate locking mechanism. As this road was the only access to the island, lengthy traffic queues resulted in summer, when the gates were closed against road traffic. Hayling Island has always been an extremely well-patronised holiday resort, complete with its holiday camp run by a nationally-known operator, and this, no doubt, contributed to the popularity of the trains during the summer season. Unfortunately, this traffic was not sustained at other times, thereby ensuring the closure of the branch, along with those at similar coastal centres.

BELOW: Langstone Bridge, shown in this view on 2nd November 1963, was the primary reason for branch closure, due to the poor condition of its wooden structure whose lack of strength also accounted for the use of the 'Terriers' with their very light axle loading. An unidentified member of the class crosses with a Hayling bound train. The signal box at the left of the picture controlled the manually-operated swing-bridge section. An abortive attempt to preserve the branch as an electrified light railway, using a redundant Blackpool Tramways vehicle, was attempted after closure, but this unlikely scheme foundered some months after the plan was first made public.

ABOVE: The labour intensive method of coaling at the Hayling Island terminus is well illustrated here in October 1963 with No. 32650 being the subject of attention. She has the larger bunker fitted to those engines used for services in the Isle of Wight and was returned to the mainland in 1937 having worked in the Island as No. W9 *Fishbourne* from 1930. Following a time as Lancing Works shunter, where No. 515S was allocated in the Departmental series, she returned to Capital Stock in 1953 and original identity. She is now preserved on the Kent & East Sussex Railway at Tenterden as their No.10 *Sutton*.

ISLE OF WIGHT LINES

RYDE-VENTNOR

OPENED:	10th September 1866
CLOSED:	18th April 1966 (Shanklin-Ventnor)

BELOW: Showing the scene which at one time greeted enthusiasts on their arrival in the Island from Portsmouth, an unidentified ex-LSWR Class 02 0-4-4T makes its way towards Ryde Pier Head against the backdrop of Ryde town, with a train from Ventnor in August 1965. The pier tramway to Ryde Esplanade occupies the tracks running behind the signal box. This section of line was formerly in the ownership of the Isle of Wight Railway, until its absorption by the Southern Railway at the 1923 Grouping. The Island was renowned for its use of pre-grouping locos and coaches, the latter ultimately being of LBSCR and SECR origin, with some lasting until December 1966 when the final remaining section from Ryde to Shanklin was closed to enable electrification work to proceed. Re-opening took place in March 1967 using redundant rolling stock from the London Underground system.

ABOVE: The token is handed to the crew of ex-LSWR 02 Class 0-4-4T No. W17 *Seaview* at Brading, before proceeding with a Ryde train in September 1966. This was the junction for the Bembridge branch, which had closed several years earlier in September 1953. By 1960, services were operated exclusively by these tanks which had all been fitted with extended bunkers. Previously, a handful of ex-LBSCR Class AIX 'Terriers' for light branch work such as the Merstone to Ventnor

West line together with EI 0-6-0 tanks for freight duties were also used. As the pattern of services altered and standardisation took effect in the post-nationalisation period, the 02s alone remained. Ryde (St. Johns Road) was the home of the Works and was virtually self-sufficient, carrying out complete overhauls on locos and rolling stock, as necessary, with the exception of heavy boiler repairs. These were dealt with at Eastleigh. (Derek Huntriss).

BELOW: Against the background of St. Boniface Down in August 1965, Class 02 No. W28 *Ashey* drifts downhill shortly after leaving Ventnor Tunnel, the summit of the line, with a Ryde train. Whilst construction was taking place, a large spring was tapped and this was subsequently diverted to provide Ventnor with water. At nearly three-quarters of a mile in length, Ventnor was the longest tunnel on the island and in the early days, trains halted for several minutes at Wroxall to allow oil lamps to be provided for each compartment. Another aspect of the island's railways, for which it was renowned, was the almost invariable cleanliness of its locomotives, this lasting until close to the final withdrawal of steam.

ABOVE: A general view of Ventnor terminus in August 1965, showing its restricted location and taken from immediately above the tunnel entrance. Note the various wooden-bodied coal wagons and carriages of pre-grouping origin berthed in the sidings. Several of the caves and openings built into the chalk cliff opposite were used for storage and as offices by local coal merchants. The terminus, like many elsewhere, suffered the disadvantage of being inconveniently situated and was a considerable height above the town it served, being 276ft above sea level. Class 02 No. W22 *Brading* awaits departure with a Ryde train.

RYDE (SMALLBROOK JUNCTION)-COWES

OPENED:	20th December 1875
CLOSED:	21st February 1966

BELOW: This view shows Class 02 No. W17 *Seaview* in September

1965 alongside the River Medina on that section of the route between Newport and Cowes (formerly Isle of Wight Central Railway), and close to Medina Wharf, with a Cowes-bound working. The railway-owned Medina Wharf was the means whereby engines and rolling stock were transferred to and from the island by means of the floating crane normally employed around Southampton Docks. Of recent times, both BR and the Preservation Society operating from Haven Street, have normally used the car ferry for this purpose!

ABOVE: Whilst the SS *United States* makes its way along Cowes Roads with a cargo of Transatlantic passengers in October 1965, the now-preserved Class 02 No. W24, by then minus nameplates and in unlined black, sits in the decaying atmosphere of Cowes terminus awaiting its return to Ryde. Note the empty sidings used in more prosperous times for the storage of coaching stock, together with further examples of wooden-bodied wagons holding domestic coal, shipped in via Medina Wharf. These were probably the last wooden wagons in normal traffic on BR tracks. Medina Wharf became predominantly a Permanent Way Department base in 1965, and handled much of the materials for the Ryde-Shanklin electrification.

FORMER LSWR LINES

BENTLEY-BORDON

OPENED:	11th December 1905
CLOSED:	16th September 1957 (Passenger)
	4th April 1966 (Freight)

BELOW: With a feather of steam escaping from its safety valves, former LSWR M7 Class 0-4-4T No. 30110 drifts down the Bordon branch on its approach to Bentley on 15th September 1957. This line formed a connection from the Farnham to Alton line to the Woolmer Instructional, later Longmoor, Military Railway. When an extension was laid from Longmoor through to Liss on the electrified Portsmouth line, the original connection assumed a lesser role, but was nonetheless retained for some years after closure to passengers, presumably as much for operational as strategic reasons. The line was built to light railway standards, all level road crossings being ungated in similar fashion to its military neighbour and provided only with cattle grids. Freight traffic on the branch in the 1950s was variously hauled by Q1 Class 0-6-0s, N Class 2-6-0s or ex-LSWR Class 700 0-6-0s. Around the commencement of the First World War, a pair of Drummond steam railcars found employment on the passenger services, sometimes in conjunction with trailer vehicles. (T. B. Owen).

ALTON-WINCHESTER JUNCTION

OPENED:	2nd October 1865
CLOSED:	5th February 1973

BELOW: Medstead and Four Marks station, now re-opened as part of the Mid-Hants Railway preservation scheme, is the subject of this view taken on 8th May 1955. M7 Class No. 30480 is shown awaiting departure to Alton with a push-pull unit composed of former LSWR stock. A pilot scheme involving the replacement of these units by 2-car 'Hampshire' DMUs was carried out in 1957, thereby enabling the virtual elimination of steam passenger operation on a regular basis. (R. C. Riley).

LEFT: The Mid-Hants line was frequently used as a diversionary route, especially when engineering work was taking place on the main line, and was able to take the heaviest motive power. It came into its own particularly at weekends, when work was being undertaken on connection with the Bournemouth electrification during 1966/67. Rebuilt Merchant Navy Class 4-6-2 No. 35029 *Ellerman Lines* is shown in this 8th May 1966 view being piloted by Standard Class 4MT 2-6-4T No. 80139 through Ropley station, now the engineering base of the preservation group, with a Waterloo-bound train. Piloting was necessary on the heavier trains because of the severe gradients on the approach to Medstead and Four Marks in each direction. This resulted in the route being known to engine crews as 'over the Alps'!

SHAWFORD JUNCTION-WINCHESTER (CHESIL)

OPENED:	1st October 1891
CLOSED:	19th September 1961 (Passenger)
	4th April 1966 (Freight)

BELOW: Whilst not strictly representative of the normal Southern branch line scene, the writer could not resist including this view of ex-LSWR B4 Class 0-4-0T No. 30096 proceeding along the former Didcot, Newbury and Southampton line with an LCGB rail tour train heading for Southampton Docks on 6th April 1963. Photographed from St. Catherines Hill it is shown alongside the River Itchen, with Winchester Cathedral discernible in the background. Whilst the line was effectively part of the GWR, or latterly Western Region system, that portion between Shawford Junction and Winchester (Chesil) Junction was operated and maintained by the LSWR from its inception. This arose from financial difficulties experienced by the original company in completing its line to Southampton, which resulted in an accommodation having to be reached with the LSWR, which provided the necessary capital for this section. Somewhat ironically the whole of the route between Newbury (Enborne Junction) and Shawford Junction was passed to the Southern Region in 1950, which thereafter retained responsibility for its operation until closure in 1960. A Saturday Only diesel service during the summer period continued until September 1961, running from Southampton to Winchester.

ANDOVER-ROMSEY (KIMBRIDGE JUNCTION)

OPENED: 6th March 1865
CLOSED: 7th September 1964 (Passenger)
                18th September 1967
                (Freight: Andover-Andover Town)

BELOW: In this rare colour picture taken in 1949 on what appears to be a beautiful Spring day, ex-LSWR K10 Class 4-4-0 No. 345, still in post-war Southern livery, ambles along this line with a train from Eastleigh. The coaching stock is also of LSWR origin, probably being a triple set.

The K10 4-4-0s, designed by Dugald Drummond and introduced in 1901, were known as 'Small Hoppers', being used for light passenger and freight duties. The class ceased to exist, along with that of its larger cousin, the L11, in the early 1950s, No. 345 being cut-up at Horley scrap sidings in November 1949. The line was chosen as one of those which would be included in the pilot Hampshire dieselisation scheme, introduced in September 1957, to which earlier reference has been made. As a result of delays in the delivery of the replacement multiple unit stock, the new interval timetable had to be introduced with a number of ex-LSWR T9 Class 4-4-0s hauling Dulleid 3-coach sets, which according to contemporary accounts, performed quite creditably on the diesel schedules for the few weeks up to early November 1957! (S. C. Townroe).

RIGHT: A scene rarely photographed in colour was that of the T9 Class undertaking freight duties. Here No. 30287 is seen in July 1958 passing Kimbridge Junction, where the secondary route from Salisbury to Eastleigh, via Romsey, merged with the Andover to Romsey line. The engine headcode indicates the route from Salisbury to Portsmouth, via Eastleigh. Awbridge Sidings, near Kimbridge Junction, became well known in 1948 as a stabling point for withdrawn locos awaiting scrapping at Eastleigh Works, which at that time in the post-war era had an excess of work. Amongst several locos lying here then were the last representatives of Adams X6 and T3 4-4-0 Classes. As luck would have it, the last T3 No. 563 was rescued for the Waterloo Station Centenary Exhibition in 1948 and has since survived as part of the NRM Collection at York. (S. C. Townroe).

WAREHAM (WORGRET JUNCTION)-SWANAGE

OPENED:	20th May 1885
CLOSED:	3rd January 1972 (Passenger)

BELOW: Against the familiar background of Corfe Castle, former SR West Country Class Light Pacific No. 34019 *Bideford* passes the station with a Saturday through train from Waterloo, via Ringwood, heading for Swanage in August 1956. The local auto-train, which would have been hauled by a class M7 0-4-4T sits in the platform awaiting clearance of the single line section whilst an unidentified Maunsell 2-6-0, probably of Class N, simmers in the sidings. Through workings from Waterloo in the Summer holiday period continued on this branch following the end of steam and the final through train ran in October 1969 hauled by a BRCW Class 33 diesel locomotive. Swanage has always been an extremely popular holiday resort, because of its location and consistently high sunshine record, and it is difficult to understand why the line was never electrified as was its Lymington neighbour. Excursions were still operated from the London and Midlands areas during the late 1960s until the lines closure, these often being composed of DMU stock in various formations, whilst ramblers' specials also ran occasionally. The regular branch service following the cessation of steam until closure, was provided by Hampshire type 3-car multiple units. (S. C. Townroe).

ABOVE: At the very end of steam working in September 1967, BR Standard Class 4MT 2-6-4T No. 80146 heads away from Furzebrook sidings with a train of china clay wagons in the Worgret Junction direction. The area was once notable for being the location of a narrow gauge mineral tramway system operated by Pike Bros., Fayle & Co., which employed locos of 0-6-0ST type to the various workings, on the unusual gauge of 2ft 8½in. Although the tramway was closed in 1956, the clay traffic survived until at least 1984. From 1978 onwards Furzebrook sidings also became the railhead for the Wych Farm oilfield, and continues to operate as such at the time of writing. The line is currently in the process of being re-opened in stages from the Swanage direction by a preservation society.

AXMINSTER-LYME REGIS

OPENED:	24th August 1903
CLOSED:	29th November 1965

BELOW: This branch on the Devon/Dorset border gained its reputation from the three ex-LSWR Adams 0415 Class 4-4-2 ('Radial') tanks whose use was dictated by the sharp gradients and severe curvature of the line along its length. Axminster was the junction station and No. 30584 is awaiting departure with the three coaches of Bulleid set 970, forming a through working from Waterloo on 11th July 1959. The branch bay platform face can be seen to the left of the locomotive, which is situated on the up main line and about to cross over on to the branch proper, which then climbed away from the station on a gradient of 1 in 80, before immediately steepening to 1 in 40 following its crossing of the main line. There was at one time a down side connection from the goods yard, but this was taken out of use in 1915.

The scene here has changed considerably since the date this view was taken, the signal box, cattle dock siding and yard having been removed long since, whilst the main line has been singled with all traffic now using the former down line. The up platform and branch bay still remain, though the passing years have resulted in their becoming considerably overgrown. The downgrading of the main line followed its takeover by the Western Region, along with other ex-Southern lines west of Salisbury in early 1963. (R. C. Riley).

RIGHT: The rather unusually styled and sited station of Combpyne is depicted here with No. 30584 leaving for Lyme Regis on 8th March 1959. This is fitted with an Adams boiler similar to that currently on No. 30583, now preserved in the guise of LSWR No. 488 on the Bluebell Railway in Sussex. Boilers of Drummond pattern, fitted with dome-mounted safety valves, were also fitted and all available boilers were interchanged periodically amongst the three class members. Anyone who had the misfortune to arrive at Combpyne on a dark winter's evening would find their way illuminated by a pair of hurricane lamps at the respective platform ends, as electricity was not available here! The presence of a Camping Coach will be noted. (R. C. Riley).

LEFT: With the rolling Dorset countryside in the background, No. 30583 stands before the single-road engine shed at Lyme Regis on 14th March 1960. This class of engine was introduced to the line from around 1916 following the failure of a variety of types, including the ex-LBSCR A1 Class 0-6-0Ts which had been purchased for the purpose, and ex-LSWR 02 Class 0-4-4Ts. With curves of ten chains radius it was found that the rigid wheelbase of the former tended to spread the track, whilst the latter suffered from both excessive flange wear and frame distortion. Notwithstanding these findings, 02 tanks were again used in 1946, due to lack of any suitable alternative, during a motive power shortage. A programme of track alterations to ease the worst curves was undertaken in the Autumn of 1960, which allowed the replacement of the long-serving Adams tanks with Standard Class 2MT 2-6-2Ts of LMS design. These operated satisfactorily until November 1963 when single unit diesel railcars took over until line closure. The line was by this time under Western Region control which took effect early in 1963. (R. C. Riley).

SIDMOUTH JUNCTION-SIDMOUTH/EXMOUTH

OPENED:	6th July 1874 (to Sidmouth)
	1st June 1903 (Tipton St. Johns-Exmouth)
CLOSED:	6th March 1967

BELOW: Standard Class 4MT 2-6-4T No. 80037 is shown leaving Sidmouth Junction with the 4.00 pm train to Sidmouth on 21st July 1963. This was also the main line junction for the route to Exmouth via Budleigh Salterton, and the first stop at which the 'Atlantic Coast Express' dropped through coaches for these coastal resorts. As with other former LSWR branches, the M7 Class 0-4-4Ts had been the mainstay of motive power for several years until the advent of the BR and LMS-designed standard classes of 2-6-2T in the 1950s. These eventually completely displaced the M7s and, along with the Standard Class 4MT 2-6-4Ts used in later years, were themselves replaced by WR diesel multiple units until line closure. Since this view was taken, the fields seen beyond the main line have been completely covered by houses forming the addition of a large new estate to the old settlement of Feniton, with the main line itself having been reduced to single track. The yard and all sidings were also removed and the station was re-opened as Feniton in May 1971 to serve the expanded population. (P. W. Gray).

RIGHT: Tipton St. Johns was the point at which the routes from Sidmouth Junction to Sidmouth and Exmouth diverged. Class M7 0-4-4T No. 30025 climbs away up the 1 in 46 gradient on 15th June 1958 with a Sidmouth train, while BR Standard Class 2MT 2-6-2T No. 84022 can just be observed waiting to regain the platform before returning with its Exmouth train. Following the simultaneous closure of both branches, the line was severed at Sidmouth Junction in June 1967, with the consequence that track lifting trains had to work from the Exmouth end. Bad flooding in East Devon during 1968 whilst this work was being undertaken, breached the track at East Budleigh as well as Newton Poppleford, isolating wagons at Tipton. For this reason the remaining sections of line and rolling stock had to be removed by road! (T. B. Owen).

LEFT: The atmosphere of a typical country station is evident here as Ivatt Class 2MT 2-6-2T No. 41321 arrives at Newton Poppleford with the 11.08 am Tipton St. Johns-Exmouth on 10th August 1963. One would imagine the provision of two platform barrows would be far in excess of any likely demand for at least the two decades before services ceased! The single siding alongside the small corrugated iron goods shed is also noted, along with its solitary goods van. This siding may have been used for delivering fertiliser or similar agricultural sundries and was taken out of use in February 1965. Camping Coaches were also a feature until these facilities were generally withdrawn throughout the system in the early 1960s. (P. W. Gray).

RIGHT: The interior of Exmouth station on 2nd November 1963 showing one of the two island platforms with Standard Class 4MT 2-6-4T No. 80041 and Ivatt Class 2MT 2-6-2T No. 41316 in front of the shed, whilst an unidentified Class 4MT 2-6-4T sits awaiting its next turn of duty. Only one platform face currently remains, and the shed area, together with the houses to the rear, have been levelled to provide a new road approach along the A376 towards the town centre. The area out of sight to the left has been incorporated into a new town car park, and the station building demolished to provide a site for the bus and coach station. There was also a Dock branch of about a half-mile in length, but this has also been removed within recent memory. (P. W. Gray).

BARNSTAPLE-ILFRACOMBE

OPENED:	1st August 1854 (to Barnstaple)
	20th July 1874 (to Ilfracombe)
CLOSED:	5th October 1970 (Ilfracombe to Barnstaple)

BELOW: Colleton Mills, between Eggesford and Kings Nympton on the Exeter-Barnstaple section, is the setting for a rather grubby No. 34069 *Hawkinge,* one of Bulleid's Battle of Britain Class Light Pacifics, heading the 2.20 pm Ilfracombe to Waterloo train on 23rd August 1963. This was a regular route for these engines and for a four-year period until its withdrawal in 1951, they were responsible for hauling a Pullman train, 'The Devon Belle', on its journey from Waterloo to Ilfracombe and return. Run during the Summer timetable, it included an observation car which necessitated it being turned on Ilfracombe's locomotive turntable. One of the coaches used is now preserved on the Dart Valley Railway. The unrebuilt Bulleid Pacifics had an unfortunate tendency to catch fire because of their oil-bath enclosed valve mechanism. Following one incident between North Tawton and Bow on the Plymouth line in 1953, involving No. 34001 *Exeter,* the engine was repainted at Exmouth Junction depot. The shade of green used was, unfortunately, far from an effective match to the existing paintwork and, coupled with the appearance of rust patches on its cladding, led to adverse comments appearing in the local city press! (P. W. Gray).

RIGHT: In the beautiful surroundings of Kings Nympton (until 1948 South Molton Road), BB Class 4-6-2 No. 34070 *Manston* chatters away with the 9.00 am Waterloo-Barnstaple Junction on the same day as the previous shot was taken. This 40-mile single line was built to broad gauge, and was worked initially by contractor Thomas Brassey with his own rolling stock before takeover and regauging by the LSWR. All intermediate stations were provided with passing loops. At the time of writing the line still remains operational for passenger traffic with a service of diesel multiple units, journeys often being combined with those between Exeter and Exmouth. Eggesford alone now retains passing facilities, whilst most stations have been reduced to 'basic railway' standards, the original buildings having been sold as private dwellings.
(P. W. Gray).

LEFT: In this unusual panoramic view, some impression can be gained of the notorious gradient from Ilfracombe to Mortehoe: just under three miles at 1 in 36, with SR N Class 2-6-0 No. 31849 piloting WC Class 4-6-2 No. 34011 *Tavistock* on 13th July 1963 on a train heading towards Exeter. The severity of the climb for enginemen lay in the fact that it commenced almost immediately from the platform end. The general layout of the station is clearly apparent, and the loco shed can be seen just behind the rear of the train and to the right of the signal gantry commanding the entrance to the station. The extensive layout of carriage sidings will be noted, these being particularly necessary in earlier years at peak holiday times, before the motor car assumed the position it has today and had deprived the railways of most of this traffic.
(T. B. Owen).

BERE ALSTON-CALLINGTON

OPENED: 2nd March 1908
CLOSED: 7th November 1966 (Gunnislake-Callington)

BELOW: Callington terminus is featured here on 18th May 1959 with Ivatt Class 2MT 2-6-2T No. 41315 preparing to leave on an early morning Plymouth working. These replaced the 02 class in 1961, having earlier displaced the PDSWJR locos in 1952. The line still provides a service as far as Gunnislake, as the road journey from Plymouth requires an additional journey of several miles in order to cross the River Tamar. This is effected on the railway by means of the twelve-arch Calstock Viaduct, an impressive and graceful example of local engineering. Passenger services are now provided by WR diesel multiple units over the shortened line, whilst freight operation ceased in February 1966. (David Soggee).

LEFT: In rather dull conditions on 20th June 1958, 02 Class 0-4-4T No. 30192 is shown nearing Callington with a mixed train, which includes one of the gated push-pull units of LSWR origin. The line was built originally by the independent Plymouth, Devonport and South Western Junction Railway to exploit the mineral wealth of the locality, and Col. H. F. Stephens (of light railway fame) was for a time its Associate Engineer. The Company owned three locomotives, manufactured by Hawthorne Leslie in 1907. One was a 0-6-0T, the others being of 0-6-2T wheel arrangement, and were absorbed into SR stock at the Grouping as Nos. 756 to 758. On their replacement on passenger work by the 02 Class in 1929, they were employed on various local duties in the Plymouth area. The last of the 0-6-2Ts was withdrawn at Eastleigh in 1957, whilst the solitary 0-6-0T, No. 756, went in 1951. This could be seen for a time at the opposite end of the system where it was used on occasions for shunting coaching stock at Clapham Junction! (T. B. Owen).

MELDON JUNCTION-PADSTOW

OPENED:	27th March 1899
CLOSED:	3rd October 1966 (Meldon Junc.-Wadebridge)
	30th January 1967 (Wadebridge-Padstow)

BELOW: Against the background of the Dartmoor Tors, with Yes Tor prominent, and taking the line from Meldon Junction towards Halwill Junction is an unidentified SR N Class 2-6-0 coupled to a mixed formation of Maunsell and Bulleid coaches, with an evening all stations working from Okehampton to Bude and Padstow in May 1964. Meldon Junction signalbox can be observed in the middle distance. The Maunsell Moguls, along with the T9 Class 4-4-0s, were the usual motive power for both passenger and freight working along the former SR routes west of Exeter, until the arrival of the Bulleid West Country Class in the mid-1940s. Later, BR Standard tanks of Class 3 2-6-2T and Class 4 2-6-4T were to make their appearance alongside these engines, although the T9 Class was finally withdrawn in 1960. (David Soggee).

ABOVE: Activity at Halwill Junction on 22nd August 1964 with five engines in view, and showing how the Standard locomotive classes had taken over from the more traditional types towards the end of steam. As Class 2MT No. 41283 waits in the left-hand bay, having arrived from Torrington, the 8.30 am Padstow-Exeter disappears in the distance headed by N Class 2-6-0 No. 31846. At the same time Standard 4MTs Nos. 80038 and 80041 wait to take out, respectively, their Bude and Okehampton trains; No. 80039 remains in the yard. Halwill Junction, being the focus for connecting services, saw periods of rural calm alternating with those of considerable activity when the relating workings arrived over a relatively short period. As with similar junctions elsewhere, the local community had developed along with the railway and existed merely to serve that need, the village of Halwill being some two miles further on. (P. W. Gray).

ABOVE: A North Cornwall pastoral scene on 22nd August 1964 with N Class 2-6-0 No. 31846 beyond Tresmeer on the line from Halwill with a five-coach rake for Wadebridge and Padstow comprising a section of the 10.35 am from Waterloo, the 'Atlantic Coast Express'. This was renowned for being composed of several through portions, each serving a coastal resort in former SR territory. Known to staff and enthusiasts alike as the 'ACE', this ran for only two seasons following the Western Region takeover and was withdrawn in September 1964. The T9 4-4-0s were particularly associated with this line over which they operated for around 40 years. (P. W. Gray).

LEFT: Class N 2-6-0 No. 31859 gets into its stride on 22nd August 1964 with an eastbound train from Otterham station, the 1.00 pm Padstow to Okehampton. The line generally ran through a sparsely inhabited but scenic part of the county. As with so many other stations along the North Cornwall line, Otterham retained much of its previous LSWR atmosphere both in terms of architecture and in the various items of station furniture, including signals. Whilst being single track, all of the intermediate stations on this stretch of railway had passing facilities in similar fashion to the Barnstaple route. Delabole was noteworthy for possessing the world's largest slate quarry at the time of the railway's construction, and the owners were sufficiently anxious to ensure quick completion of their rail outlet that they presented three-quarters of a mile of land to the company free of charge in 1883! (P. W. Gray).

HALWILL JUNCTION-TORRINGTON

OPENED:	27th July 1925
CLOSED:	27th February 1965 (Passenger)
	31st August 1982
	(Freight: Meeth-Barnstaple)

BELOW: With its single Bulleid coach, Ivatt 2-6-2T No. 41312 stands for a few minutes at Hatherleigh on the North Devon & Cornwall Junction Light Railway with a train for Halwill on 23rd June 1962. There would appear to be around five members of railway staff present, which underlines the doubtful economics of running passenger services on such rural lines, where employees were likely to outnumber passengers by a considerable margin. It was mainly the china clay traffic, originating from the quarries of Peters, Marland and Meeth, which enabled the line to survive, and this continued following passenger withdrawal. It was for this reason that it had originally been built under Southern Railway auspices in 1925, partly replacing an earlier 3ft gauge mineral tramway. Until the early 1950s Maunsell rebuilds of the LBSCR Stroudley E1 Class, reclassified E1/R, and being fitted with extended bunkers and a radial truck as 0-6-2Ts, were employed here, often working mixed trains. Some of these saw out their final days as banking engines, assisting on the notorious incline between Exeter (St. Davids) and Exeter Central. (R. C. Riley).

LEFT: A month following official closure, Ivatt 2-6-2Ts Nos. 41206 and 41291 approach Hole station with the RCTS/PRC 'Exmoor Ranger' railtour on 27th March 1965. The remote nature of the countryside in this area is apparent. The Ivatt 2-6-2Ts were the line's regular motive power from 1957 onwards when they took over from the E1/R 0-6-2Ts, which had replaced the elderly Adams 4-4-0s that first worked the line. Following passenger closure, and after a brief time of diesel railcar operation, the line was shut completely between Halwill and Meeth, the northern section being retained to serve the various china clay workings. Staff were specially retained on the section from which traffic was withdrawn, to enable the 'Exmoor Ranger' to pass.

DUNMERE JUNCTION-WENFORD BRIDGE

OPENED: 30th September 1834
CLOSED: November 1983

BELOW: The china clay traffic as with other Cornish lines was the main reason behind the building of the goods only branch to Wenford Bridge. Here, ex-LSWR Beattie 2-4-0WT No. 30585 leaves the terminal for Dunmere Junction with a train of loaded wagons on 13th July 1961. Initially the line had been intended for working by horses, but was locomotive operated from its inception in 1834, being the first of its type in Cornwall. The Beattie well tanks were introduced to the line in 1898, and three of the type continued to operate it until their replacement by former GWR '1366' Class 0-6-0PTs in 1962. Their basic design originated in the 1860s, when they had been introduced for suburban passenger traffic from Waterloo. They underwent many successive rebuildings, receiving boilers of both Adams and Drummond design in the intervening years, and most similarities (other than wheel arrangement) to their initial appearance eventually became difficult to detect. Along with Stroudley's 'Terriers' they probably hold the record for longevity of service of any main line type. Following the displacement of steam, BR 350hp diesel shunters of Class 08 worked the line until closure. (P. W. Gray).

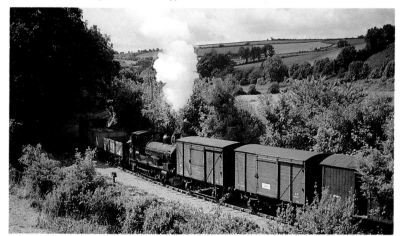

RIGHT: Beattie Well Tank No. 30586 stands in front of Wadebridge goods shed whilst acting as station pilot on 13th July 1961. This engine differed from the two remaining members of the class in possessing square-outline splashers, as compared with their rounded profile. This was the sole member of the class to be scrapped following withdrawal in 1962. An unusual duty for the station pilot in July 1954 was a passenger trip around midday, from Wadebridge to Padstow and return. This came about in order to allow sufficient re-fuelling time at Wadebridge for the 02 tank then employed on the Bodmin-Padstow service. The practice was discontinued the following month as a result of the additional time required for engine changeover. A further appearance on this duty was recorded in July 1962, shortly before their withdrawal. No. 30585 is currently preserved at Quainton Road in Buckinghamshire, whilst No. 30587 from the NRM Collection is on loan to the Dart Valley Railway Museum at Buckfastleigh. (R. C. Riley).

The desolate and windswept nature of the landscape at the Thames Estuary end of the Hundred of Hoo is well-epitomised by this final view of an unidentified H Class 0-4-4T leaving Stoke Junction for Allhallows-on-Sea on 18th November 1961. The chimneys and storage tanks of the Isle of Grain oil refinery can be discerned in the distance. (David Soggee).

BIBLIOGRAPHY

The following have proved especially helpful:
History of the Southern Railway Dendy Marshall/R. W. Kidner Ian Allan 1963
Passengers No More G. Daniels/L. Dench Ian Allan 1973
The Axminster to Lyme Regis Railway E. J. Rose Kingfisher 1982
Various issues of the *'Railway Observer'* (RCTS)